ANCIENT
CIVILIZATIONS

ANCIENT
CHINA

BY EMILY ROSE OACHS

BLASTOFF!
DISCOVERY

BELLWETHER MEDIA   MINNEAPOLIS, MN

Blastoff! Discovery launches a new mission: reading to learn. Filled with facts and features, each book offers you an exciting new world to explore!

This edition first published in 2020 by Bellwether Media, Inc.

No part of this publication may be reproduced in whole or in part without written permission of the publisher.
For information regarding permission, write to Bellwether Media, Inc.,
Attention: Permissions Department,
6012 Blue Circle Drive, Minnetonka, MN 55343.

Library of Congress Cataloging-in-Publication Data

Names: Oachs, Emily Rose, author.
Title: Ancient China / by Emily Rose Oachs.
Description: Minneapolis, MN : Bellwether Media, Inc., 2020. |
   Series: Blastoff! Discovery: ancient civilizations |
   Includes bibliographical references and index. |
   Audience: Ages 7-13 | Audience: Grades 4-6 |
   Summary: "Engaging images accompany information about
   ancient China. The combination of high-interest subject matter and
   narrative text is intended for students in grades 3 through 8"–
   Provided by publisher.
Identifiers: LCCN 2019036012 (print) | LCCN 2019036013 (ebook)
   | ISBN 9781644871744 (library binding) | ISBN 9781618918581
   (paperback) | ISBN 9781618918505 (ebook)
Subjects: LCSH: China–Civilization–Juvenile literature.
Classification: LCC DS721 .O23 2020 (print) | LCC DS721 (ebook)
   | DDC 931–dc23
LC record available at https://lccn.loc.gov/2019036012
LC ebook record available at https://lccn.loc.gov/2019036013

Editor: Kate Moening   Designer: Jeffrey Kollock

Printed in the United States of America, North Mankato, MN.

TABLE OF CONTENTS

A DAY IN THE FIELDS

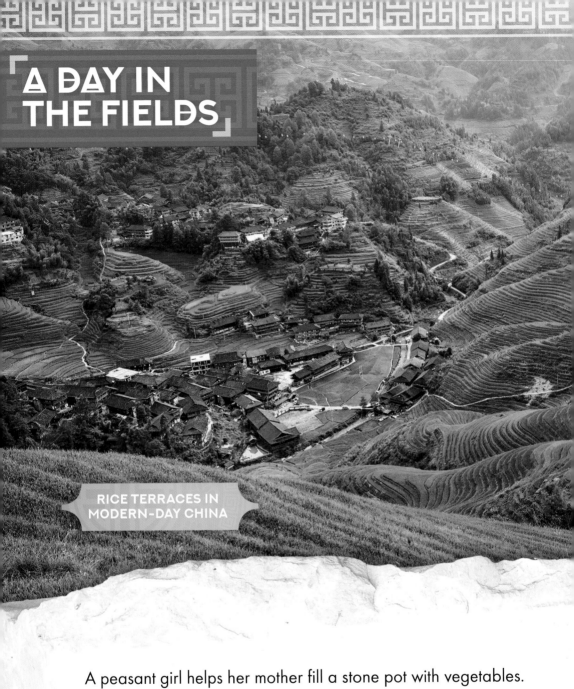

RICE TERRACES IN MODERN-DAY CHINA

A peasant girl helps her mother fill a stone pot with vegetables. She places it over the fire in their hut. The vegetables will cook while they work in the fields.

HARVESTING RICE

They meet the girl's father in the **paddy**. Water floods between the rows of rice. The girl bends to pull weeds. Her stomach growls as she works. But she knows there will be a delicious meal waiting at home. It will be time to eat after a day of farming in ancient China!

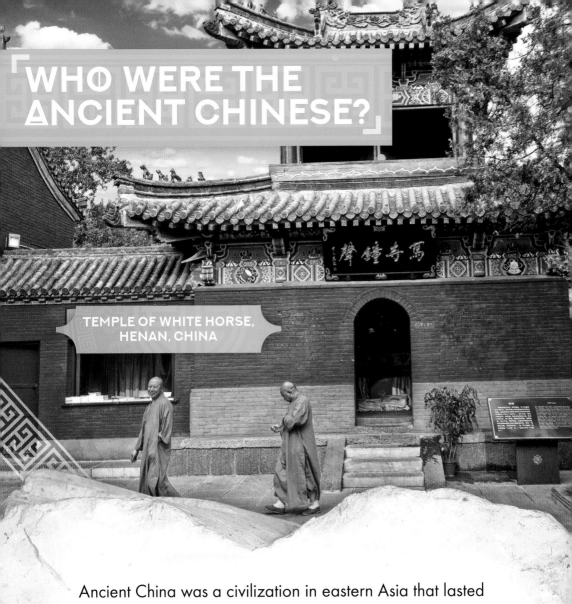

TEMPLE OF WHITE HORSE, HENAN, CHINA

Ancient China was a civilization in eastern Asia that lasted more than 1,800 years. Its history is divided into **dynasties**. Ancient China began with the Shang dynasty around 1600 BCE. The Han dynasty's fall in 220 CE brought its end.

Ancient China called itself *Zhongguo*, or "Middle Empire." It reached its peak of **culture** and power during the Han dynasty. Its borders reached present-day Vietnam, North Korea, and Central Asia. At its height, ancient China had around 60 million people.

ANCIENT CHINA'S DYNASTIES

SHANG
1600 TO 1046 BCE

KNOWN FOR
- creation of bronze items such as weapons
- early Chinese writing

ZHOU
1046 TO 256 BCE

KNOWN FOR
- development of Confucianism and Taoism
- Mandate of Heaven
- iron
- plows pulled by oxen

QIN
221 TO 207 BCE

KNOWN FOR
- unification of China
- beginning of the Great Wall
- terra-cotta army
- books burned by order of Shihuangdi

HAN
206 BCE TO 220 CE

KNOWN FOR
- golden age of culture and literature
- imperial academy created to prepare people for government jobs
- paper, kites, and sundials
- Silk Road trading route

Ancient China's landscape featured the Yangtze, Yellow, and many other rivers. They offered easy travel for a growing civilization. They also provided rich soil for farming.

Advances in agriculture strengthened ancient China. Iron plows and wheelbarrows helped farmers perform everyday tasks more easily. Each season, farmers chose different crops to plant in their fields. This rotation kept the soil healthy. Chinese farming practices made more food available as China's population grew.

HAN DYNASTY ANCIENT CHINA

KEY ■ Early Han dynasty

YELLOW RIVER

YANGTZE RIVER

N
W   E
S

YANGTZE RIVER

Ancient China is remembered for its beautiful art, military strength, and religious **philosophies**. For centuries, China was largely separated from other large civilizations. This allowed China's culture to grow freely without outside forces.

PAPER

Invented around 105 CE, paper quickly became widely used throughout China.

HOW PAPER HELPED ANCIENT CHINA GROW

- ☑ low price made it easier for more people to learn to read
- ☑ made it easier to record information and history
- ☑ allowed wider spread of information
- ☑ enabled first paper money
- ☑ used for important military maps
- ☑ brought in wealth from trading

CHINESE INVENTIONS

Ancient China produced many "firsts." The first compasses and the first paper date back to the Han dynasty. Kites were also invented in ancient China. They were used in warfare as long ago as 200 BCE!

GREAT WALL OF CHINA

Natural **barriers** kept China separate from the world. Deserts protected the north. The Pacific Ocean blocked enemy attacks to the east. The Himalayas guarded the west. During later dynasties, the **Great Wall** also protected China from outsiders. Its construction began during the Qin dynasty.

HOW THE ANCIENT CHINESE RULED

KING MU OF THE ZHOU DYNASTY

Monarchs called emperors ruled ancient China. Each emperor belonged to a dynasty. The role of emperor was passed along to the emperor's oldest son. The Zhou was ancient China's longest dynasty. It lasted about 800 years.

The Zhou introduced a belief called the **Mandate** of Heaven. The Mandate said emperors were chosen by the gods. The gods would select only moral rulers. Unworthy emperors would be replaced with someone more moral. For centuries, a philosophy called Confucianism guided the morals of emperors.

CONFUCIUS

WHO IS CONFUCIUS? highly respected philosopher

WHEN DID HE LIVE? around 551 to 479 BCE, during the Zhou dynasty

WHERE DID HE LIVE? grew up near China's eastern coast

WHAT IS HE KNOWN FOR?

- concerned with creating an ordered society
- believed in moral lives, good manners, and following social rules to achieve order
- encouraged finding wisdom in the past and in ancestors to live morally
- followers collected his teachings into a book called the Analects

WHY IS HE IMPORTANT?

- his lessons formed the foundation of Confucianism
- his ideas about morals guided emperors for centuries
- schools taught all students to live by Confucian ideas
- family, education, social order, and manners are still important in Chinese culture today

13

The Zhou dynasty fell around 256 BCE. After that, separate Chinese kingdoms fought for many years. In 221 BCE, Shihuangdi ended the Warring States Period. His powerful army brought China under one ruler. This became the Qin dynasty.

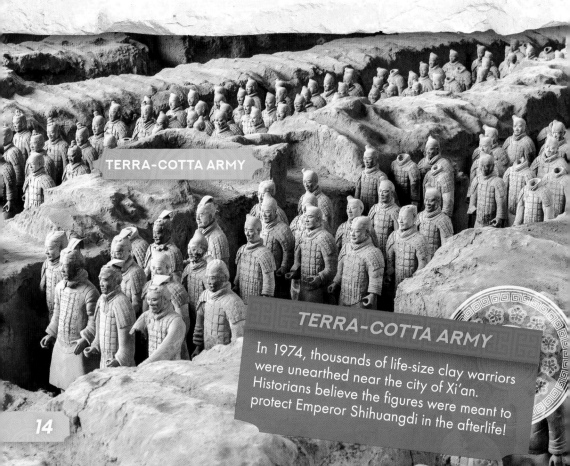

TERRA-COTTA ARMY

TERRA-COTTA ARMY

In 1974, thousands of life-size clay warriors were unearthed near the city of Xi'an. Historians believe the figures were meant to protect Emperor Shihuangdi in the afterlife!

THINK ABOUT IT

How could a route like the Silk Road help spread ideas and religions to distant places?

Emperor Shihuangdi controlled China with military force. Later leaders used trade to maintain power. Around 130 BCE, a large system of trade routes grew through China. This was called the Silk Road. It allowed the trade of goods and ideas between China and the West. The Silk Road added to China's power and wealth.

CRAFTSMEN WORKING

By the Han dynasty, ancient Chinese society was divided into four classes. The most highly respected were the rulers, nobles, and **scholars**. Next were peasant farmers who worked the nobles' land. Third were craftspeople, and last came traders.

Education was very important. Usually, only wealthy men learned to read and write. During the Han dynasty, schools opened to train students in philosophy. These students took challenging tests to earn prized government jobs. Government jobs were one way people could move to higher social classes.

Men in ancient China supported their families with jobs outside the home. Women raised children, cooked, and cleaned the house. Most ancient Chinese were peasant farmers. The children helped their parents tend the fields.

Rice and vegetables were served at almost every meal. Sometimes fish was on the menu. Servants prepared the food in wealthy families. Tea was also popular. People drank it as a medicine and to relax.

TEA

SILK WEAVING

BELIEFS AND CULTURE

STATUE OF BUDDHA

The ancient Chinese practiced many religions. In the Shang dynasty, the Chinese had many gods. Each oversaw a different part of life. People also worshipped their **ancestors**. They hoped their ancestors would bring good fortune.

The Zhou dynasty saw new religious philosophies. Confucianism highlighted moral living and social order. It taught that firm social rules created a strong society. Taoism encouraged balance with the universe. It taught people to accept the natural way of things. These philosophies guided politics and everyday life. By 100 CE, the Silk Road brought Buddhism from India.

CONFUCIANISM AND TAOISM

ORIGIN ■ 6th to 5th century BCE

IMPORTANT TEXTS ■ the Analects

CONFUCIANISM

FOUNDER

■ Confucius, also known as Kongzi

BELIEFS

- morality and rituals important to maintain social order
- inner morals directly affect world events
- family is very important
- leaders and teachers should set an example by acting with honor and kindness

ORIGIN ■ 6th century BCE

IMPORTANT TEXTS ■ Daodejing, Zhuangzi

TAOISM

BELIEFS

- universal energy present in all things, called the *tao*
- accepting the tao brings balance and harmony
- creating laws to change or control the tao is harmful
- balance between universe's opposite forces shown using the yin-yang sign

FOUNDER ■ Laozi

The earliest known Chinese writing appeared during the Shang dynasty. Fortune-tellers wrote special characters onto animal bones. These characters stood for words. The bones were used to see the future.

CHINESE CHARACTERS OVER TIME

Written Chinese characters continued to change over the centuries. See if you can spot similarities and differences!

SHANG

human   tree

water   fire

cloud   horse

ZHOU

human   tree

water   fire

cloud   horse

QIN & HAN

人 human   木 tree

水 water   火 fire

雲 cloud   馬 horse

MODERN

人 human   木 tree

水 water   火 fire

云 cloud   马 horse

THINK ABOUT IT

Why might an emperor order books destroyed?

ZHOU DYNASTY WRITING

Written Chinese continued to develop over time. Books of poetry, military planning, and philosophy came out of the Zhou dynasty. Many of these were lost when Shihuangdi gave orders to destroy them. The Han dynasty worked to recover the lost books. Later, the Han began keeping its own historical records. These were written on silk or wood strips until paper was invented.

SHANG DYNASTY
BRONZE CONTAINER

Ancient Chinese art often featured metals. Artists created fancy containers from bronze. Some featured dragons or animal faces. The Shang and Zhou dynasties often used bronze containers in religious **rituals**. Rituals also often featured a valuable stone called jade. Artists carved it into animals, jewelry, and small masks.

Artists created paintings to illustrate their philosophies and show themselves to be moral people. During the Han dynasty, the art of **calligraphy** developed. The Chinese treasured the balance of structure and emotion in each written character.

CALLIGRAPHY

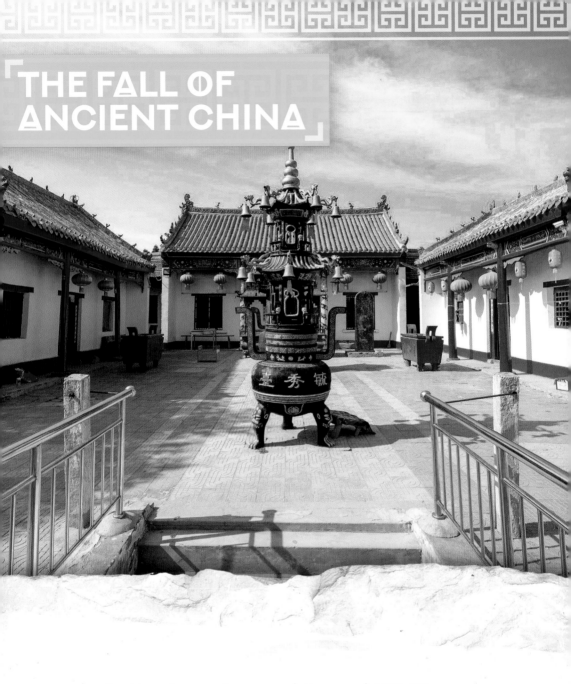

THE FALL OF ANCIENT CHINA

The Han dynasty began to fail around 100 CE.
The government was filled with dishonest leaders.
Many young rulers rapidly came and went. **Rebellions**
weakened the empire. Military leaders fought for control.

Finally, in 220 CE, Han emperor Xiandi gave up his rule. His power was too weak to control warring areas. It marked the end of the Han dynasty. China sunk into a violent period known as the Three Kingdoms. Ancient China had fallen.

ANCIENT CHINA TIMELINE

221 BCE
Shihuangdi unifies China, marking the start to the Qin dynasty

ABOUT 105 CE
paper is invented

ABOUT 130 BCE
trade begins along the Silk Road, which connects China to the Mediterranean Sea

220 CE
the fall of the Han dynasty leads to the division of the empire into three separate kingdoms

1046 BCE
the longest dynasty, the Zhou, begins its reign of almost 800 years

1600 BCE
the Shang dynasty begins

Today, China has a population of nearly 1.4 billion people. Most are **descendants** of ancient Chinese. These descendants call themselves the Han people, after the ancient dynasty. Modern Chinese share many **traditions** with their ancestors. The roots of Chinese New Year celebrations date to the Shang dynasty.

GUIYANG, CHINA

Ancient China left a long legacy. Calligraphy, ancestor **veneration**, and ancient philosophies live on. Modern society also still uses paper, compasses, and other Chinese inventions. People around the world owe much to this ancient civilization!

THINK ABOUT IT

What does the practice of ancestor worship show about how the ancient Chinese viewed family?

GLOSSARY

ancestors—relatives who lived long ago

barriers—things that block movement from one place to another

calligraphy—beautiful or stylized handwriting

culture—the beliefs, arts, and ways of life in a place or society

descendants—people related to a person or group of people who lived at an earlier time

dynasties—lines of rulers that come from the same family

Great Wall—a system of walls built along ancient China's northern border for protection; construction on the Great Wall occurred from the Qin dynasty though the end of the Ming dynasty in 1644 CE.

mandate—a formal order

monarchs—people who rule a kingdom or empire

paddy—a flooded field in which rice is grown

philosophies—ideas about knowledge, the way people should live, and the meaning of life

rebellions—efforts by many people to change the government or leader of a country, often through protests or violence

rituals—religious ceremonies or practices

scholars—people who are very educated

traditions—customs, ideas, or beliefs handed down from one generation to the next

veneration—the act of showing deep respect

TO LEARN MORE

AT THE LIBRARY

Bell, Samantha S. *Ancient China*. Lake Elmo, Minn.: Focus Readers, 2020.

Demi. *Confucius: Great Teacher of China*. New York, N.Y.: Shen's Books, 2016.

Slepian, Curtis. *You Are There! Ancient China: 305 BC*. Huntington Beach, Calif.: Teacher Created Materials, 2016.

ON THE WEB

FACTSURFER

Factsurfer.com gives you a safe, fun way to find more information.

1. Go to www.factsurfer.com.

2. Enter "ancient China" into the search box and click 🔍.

3. Select your book cover to see a list of related web sites.

INDEX